Claire,
Thank you
for sharing your
story.
Much love—
Ky

8
Ways of Being

How to Motivate
Yourself to Live Happy
and Free Every Day

Kyra Oliver

Dear Thomas

Thank you

Thank you for your
kind love

love

Design by Kyra Oliver

www.facebook/kyraoliver
www.instagram.com/kyraoliver

www.yourownutopia.com
Lifestyle That Feels Good™

Library of Congress Cataloging-in-Publication Data

Oliver Kyra

8 Ways of Being: How to Motivate Yourself to Live Happy and Free Every Day/ Kyra Oliver.

ISBN-13:978-1986007498
ISBN-10:1986007499

1. Fitness 2. Wellness 3. Health 4. Personal Development
5. Self-help 6. Lifestyle 7. Education 8. Psychology

for my sweet little boy, Hayes.

you have given Mommy the biggest gift

in the

world,

the gift of

y.o.u.

01.23.02

to

06.11.02

Testimonials

I have worked with Kyra for a number of years and love how she has taken the tragedy of losing her 4 1/2-month-old baby boy towards empowering others to live a goal-inspired lifestyle of positive thinking and good health. Her passion for her purpose of making a difference in this world shines through with authenticity in this motivational piece of work. What a gift she has given us! I look forward to seeing what's next.

Dr. Josh Axe
Author of bestseller "Eat Dirt," owner of the
#1 wellness website in the country, doctor of
natural medicine and clinical nutritionist

Kyra puts love into action in such a powerful way, reminding us, no matter the circumstances, to keep pushing forward. She is such a beacon of light.

Robyn McCord O'Brien
The "Erin Brockovich" of foods, bestselling author
of The Unhealthy Truth, public speaker

A message to the reader

This book is FOR you. I have included an exercise at the end of each chapter so that you can create your own workshop of progress and development that will guide you into a life of happiness and freedom. There is a place in the back of this book that is designated for these exercises. Do each exercise that I have provided. Refer back to your notes daily. Use the journal section too. This is where things become real!

This book is intended to provide support and fresh, positive ways of thinking so that you can live a life of happiness and freedom, a true gift.

Any reader should consult with a professional as needed. I, Kyra Oliver, do not claim to be a doctor and do not take responsibility for how one applies this book. However, I hope that the application becomes a daily encouragement. Ultimately, I am here to support you positively and in an inspiring way with the contents of this book.

I am a wellness influencer, entrepreneur, author, writer, philanthropist, coach, fitness instructor, ultra runner, and triathlete. I am passionate, from the inside out, about my community and my environment.

This publication contains the opinions and ideas of the author. For more information about me, see my bio at the end of this book.

Thank You

I have so many people to thank for believing in me, encouraging me and helping me to choose a positive way of thinking and living. I truly hope that I have not left anyone out, but please know that you all are in my heart at all times.

Special thanks to God; my late mother, Vicki; my father, Carson; my brother, Darren; Pat and the kids; my late brother, Greg; Danny and Harlena; and all of my family; Dr. Josh Axe; Mary; Meredith; Catherine; Ted Wallof; Donna Suro; Pastor Mark Foreman; Pastor Ryan Pfieffer and his wife, Jenni Lee Crocker; John Homs; Jamye; Will; Emily; Meghan; Ginny; Gina; Ethan; Joe; Jason; Gail; Rick and Stacey; Chris D.; Krisstel, Chris F.; Jason, Lindsay, and all of CCRB staff; CCRB Members; Bill and Stacy; Alex; Les and Si; Bob Loghry and the entire Tennessee crew; all my coaches; Graced by Grit; Muir Energy; Kevin, Shoko, Jeff H., George, Jason, SMJ, Liliana, Kirsten, Lisa, Kristi, Stephanie, Veronica, Parisa, Carolyn, and all the Pannikin Runners!

Thank you to my friend and author, Lisa Tyre, for proofing and being such an inspiration, and to Matthew Potts for being one of my editors and a life-encourager.

Contents

Introduction

I received the worst phone call imaginable. "Hayes isn't breathing," said the voice on the other end. I rushed to the hospital. They would not let me see him. They said he wasn't there yet.

Not there?

I would have gone where he was.

I was hysterical and they threatened to escort me out if I did not calm down.

CALM DOWN?

I just received a phone call that my precious baby is not breathing; my precious baby—my entire existence in this world, a love that I have never felt in my life; a love so strong and powerful—nothing one can really understand until they have a child...and they wanted me to calm down.

I calmed down. I did not want to be taken out of the hospital.

Moments later, I was taken to a room. A dark room. I recall a couple of lamps and a few friends already in the room. I found this to be bizarre. How did they know? Did they know something I did not?

I realized that this nightmare was my life.

The hospital chaplain walked into the room.

The lights went out.

My life became a very, very dark gray.

I asked to go to my son. They warned me that they were trying to revive him.

REVIVE HIM?

Horror became more horror. I walked in to find my son with tubes everywhere and about five people working to bring him back to life. A part of me felt that he already died, but they wanted me to see their efforts so they started working on him to appease me. We moms know these things sometimes.

I held his hand. Cold. Blue. Lifeless.

I talked to him "Hayes, please come back. Please, Mommy is here. I love you."

He wasn't coming back.

They looked at me and told me that if he were to come back, he would have extensive brain damage.

I cry as I write this.

They left me with one woman in the room. I asked to hold him. She expressed that they typically were not allowed to do that.

WHAT?

I cannot hold my baby. Hold MY baby one last time. She told me to go ahead, but quickly.

He was heavy. So heavy in my arms.

He left me.

What happened? He was gone. That's all I knew.

My son had died of SIDS (Sudden Infant Death Syndrome). That meant we do not know why he died. So we call it SIDS.

Sharing that story is crucial to everything I do now and for the rest of my life. To have been given the gift of losing my son—yes, I would rather him be here, but the gift is what I see now. The gift is what I went through after I lost him, though I could not see it for a very long time.

The gift is what I am sharing with you now, which is a gift TO you.

I had to hit rock bottom in a lot of areas—almost every single area of my life—to get here. I went through so many years of not listening. I allowed who I am to be lost in the emotion of it all. So many people would think this is OK—I mean, wow, I lost my little boy whom I held in my arms.

But the loss went further. While the loss of Hayes is pretty much as far as it can go, I spiraled. Many did not know. I was good at toughing it out. I was good at keeping myself up and motivated. But behind closed doors, I was hurting so much that it nearly took me to a darkness that I could not escape.

THAT is when the process truly began.

It took me a very long time to understand love and kindness in its truest sense. It took me so long to be able to write to you, with complete confidence, owning my mistakes and committing to learning from them.

I will never be perfect in the sense of the definition we all know, but to me, perfect is doing your best by using what you learn and never giving up. I used to have days that were so difficult and unbearable. I now have short moments that I have learned to use as a way to see something good—an opportunity to be better. A way to give to others.

"8 Ways of Being" is an expression of how you can use your thinking and mindset to capture opportunities in life. Through that, you will find so much happiness. For many long years, I thought I could not find that happiness. But I kept pushing, and I started paying attention to my choices.

I am sharing this because I truly want YOU to have a fulfilled life. I share things about myself, not for attention, but so that you can relate to it in some way. So that you can see that I am genuinely sharing my heart and soul. I want you to take every smidgen of that emotion and use it to power you up.

I want you to be happy. The more happiness you exude, the more you will see from others. We, as life on this earth, are responsible. It changes you.

I love you as tears of joy for you fall upon my cheeks.

And this is why I am sharing. MY WHY is my son, Hayes. He taught me that I needed to live a love-filled life of kindness through a humble heart. You, too, may have endured (and still are in) a lot of pain, and the exhaustion of it all is wearing on you. I have been in that dark place. I get it. The point is this: I am sharing what you need to know, to not only survive but to THRIVE! What is YOUR WHY?

#1
Love

A day finally came when I decided to not
allow that pain to be a part of me anymore.
I accepted and forgave. That moment
gave me freedom—freedom to love!

#1
Love

When you're in pain, when you've suffered a loss and trauma, when you feel that perhaps you've been wronged by someone—even opening up social media and seeing all of the perfect lives everyone else seems to lead—it is almost a reflex to view the world through cynical eyes. The tendency is to build a wall around your heart. But that wall can make your heart harden to a point that will blind you to the amazing love and kindness that exists. That hardened heart will cut you sharper than any knife causing hate and anger to engulf your life.

However, nothing ever became better through hate—ever.

Choose to love. That doesn't mean you have to like everything that happens or every behavior that you see. But if you fill your heart with love, your stress will diminish and your zest for life will consume your every breath!

I struggled for many years because I did not always have the best influences in my life. Many negative, pessimistic minds surrounded me. I didn't receive much encouragement for many young years of my life. Instead, it was faults, finger pointing, and defense. So I had to lift myself up. It took work to learn how to see and feel love. It even took work to realize how my own behavior was being affected.

Give love; get love.

Regardless of any situation you may be in, this is what happens: **Give love; get love.** Even if the love is simply something that you feel in your heart throughout your whole day. Kind thoughts instead of always assuming the worst. Positive instead of negative. Or a small gift to someone—maybe someone you don't even know.

Now let's look at the other side. What do you think happens if you give hate? Yep, you get hate. You will live a life of frustration and anger that is building up inside of you. Is that really the way you want to live? Who wants to go around being mad and angry all the time? And with that attitude, you are definitely not going to attract love of any kind.

An important perspective that we have to remember is that not everyone is in the same beautiful place that we may be—not yet. If you take a step back and think about your past, you will probably see that there were many times when you were not at your best. I recall this period of my life, and it was far longer than it should have been—years, in fact. But, over time, I finally opened my eyes to what LIFE really is. I began making better choices by loving others and appreciating what I have.

Another behavioral element that will help you feel and give love is to forgive.

I have a very special person in my life who continued to hurt me over and over. The hurt was so deep that I struggled to stop thinking about it. I'd cry when I felt the pain. I had so much anger and hurt because it had affected my behavior and the way I valued myself.

After many years of trying so hard to reshape this person into what I wanted, I finally realized that I was going at it the wrong way. It was about me. I wanted it my way. Yes, this person did and said things that were inappropriate; however, I don't have to like it. I can remove myself from those things and love them as they are. They love me deeply but they have no idea of the negative impact they have had on me for years. My expectations simply lead to more pain.

A day finally came when I decided to not allow that pain to be a part of me anymore. I accepted and forgave. That moment gave me freedom—freedom to love!

We define love in many ways, from loving family and friends to a romantic partner. But love is also defined as appreciation for all things. It is a mindset, and it takes practice to live it and receive it (unless you were raised to think this way).

Another side to love that is the most important: Love offers peace in your heart.

full on peacefulness

Love contains the most beautiful peacefulness you can imagine. Do you know what that feels like? You can try feeling it just by meditating. You can meditate and pray on that peacefulness. Using deep breaths, you can bring your mind and body to a sense of peacefulness about whatever is around you.

I use this technique when I find myself feeling stress. I recognize that I don't want that stress. I wish it away and ask for love, kindness, and peacefulness using calming thoughts and deep breaths. I pray on it. I meditate on it. In most cases, the peacefulness comes to me very quickly. Then I hold on to it.

A love-filled body and mind will set you apart from anything and anyone. Nothing can break through because you choose to love. That moment of choice will change your heart forever.

EXERCISE
New Way of Being: #1 Love

1. List 5 things you are grateful for.

2. Recall an incident when you felt frustrated and annoyed. Write it down. What happened? How did you feel (angry, like you wanted to cry or scream, disrespected)? What did you do? Are you happy with how you handled it?

Now, imagine that same feeling. How would you prefer to handle the situation? For example, can you think about what you are grateful for in the moment? Perhaps something at work really frustrates you. Can you think of something like "I am grateful I have this job so that I can feed my family?"

Another example: Perhaps a partner or someone you are dating has said something to upset you. For all you know, they did not mean it the way you are thinking, but nonetheless, you are upset. What is causing this feeling? Write it down. Can you stop? Can you step back? Can you go to a positive way of thinking about this? We often end up in a cesspool of emotion that builds and builds over nothing. You have to stop that snowball of recklessness. You can consciously stop it by being aware.

3. Practice this: The next time someone frustrates you, instead of feeling angry with them, take a moment to pause. Think compassionate and empathetic thoughts towards that person. Pray for patience, and hope that they, too, will find peace and love in their hearts one day. Remember that you do not want to live in anger. Instead, you want to experience peace and love. Remember, to get love, you have to give love.

4. Take several deep breaths while thinking about how YOU want to be as a person, how YOU want to think as a person, how YOU want to feel at this moment and after this moment. Write it down.

5. Think of four gifts of love that you can share over the next month—one per week (or more if you like). Write it down. It can be a donation, helping someone with a ride, listening to a friend in need, cooking dinner for your family, or simply saying hello with a smile to everyone you see...anything at all. After each item, write down exactly how you are going to achieve it. Include any steps required.

#2
Physical Fitness

A friend recently asked me what running does for me. I told him that it saved my life. He asked how. I explained that it gives me something to look forward to. I have new friends, personal goals, and a constant in my life; but I also used it as an escape for many years.

#2
Physical Fitness

When we're depressed, the most natural thing in the world is to curl up in the fetal position and do nothing. You've been through a lot so you have thoughts like, "What's the use?" But this is where the laws of physics kick in—objects at rest tend to stay at rest, objects in motion tend to stay in motion. The simple fact that you are reading this book is an indication that YOU CAN DO IT AND WANT TO DO IT! So, if you aren't already or you are sort of halfway exercising, as in not consistently and without a lot of effort, you have to bring physical fitness into your life on a regular basis and with intention. Period.

Physical fitness is vital to living a positive life. Why? You have to feel good to love; being fit and healthy helps you do that. If you don't feel good, how can you give to others in the way that we all need to?

You can't.

●●●●●●●●

I learned this in a really hard way. I went through one of the toughest tragedies a person can face. I lost my baby boy when he was only four and a half months old. I was beyond devastated and could not even believe it had happened. But something to point out is that I had a bit of a partying lifestyle through college, and I continued to enjoy alcohol a bit more than I should have. I was still a very responsible business owner, but when I got home, I enjoyed my red wine and, on the weekends, I enjoyed it even more. I did not drink when I was pregnant, but the interest in doing so was there after my son was born. I was breastfeeding, so it wasn't an option quite yet. Then, my son died so unexpectedly and the devastation covered me like a thick, super-heavy blanket that I could not lift off of me. Alcohol stepped back into my life. My mind could not understand what had happened and could only do so much—simply getting out of bed was difficult.

●●●●●●●●

It was that tragedy that led me to the realization that if I didn't take care of myself, I was going have an even tougher go at it. I saw that I needed to stop my drinking. Fortunately, I had spent a period of my life with a friend who did not drink. I decided I could stop drinking too. For me, it was no big deal, and boy was I glad. (Honestly, I was not sure how I would feel about going cold-turkey.) But quitting changed my life and helped me to deal with the loss of my son.

Once drinking was out of the picture, exercise became a part of my life, but in ways that I had never imagined. It led to good health, good friends, amazing adventures, and a lifestyle that made me feel great.

That doesn't mean all the pain from my tragedy (and much more) is gone, but fitness has helped me deal with the pain. It has helped me learn to live with my loss in healthier ways. And though I stopped drinking many years ago, I occasionally have a glass of wine with a meal. However, I have no interest or need to use alcohol to create a state of euphoria. For that, I am grateful.

＊＊＊＊＊＊＊＊

I want to make a side note here. A friend recently asked me what running does for me. I told him that it saved my life. He asked how. I explained that it gives me something to look forward to. I have new friends, personal goals, and a constant in my life, but I also used it as an escape for many years. This can be good to a certain extent, but for me, I pushed it too far for a very long time. I discovered I was a pretty good runner and got so into it that I ignored the healthy side of it. I found myself with a lot of injuries. I told my friend that I had used it to mask my pain. THAT IS NOT WHAT YOU NEED TO DO. That is a mistake and I learned this lesson the hard way.

＊＊＊＊＊＊＊＊

It took me years to learn some things because I did not want to listen. You've gotta listen. It isn't healthy to cover up the pain. You have to deal with it, acknowledge it, and embrace it (which doesn't mean you have to like it) so that it becomes a peaceful part of your being.

It's sort of like saying, "OK, I get why I feel that anger or pain. I'm going to take a few deep breaths, accept it, and be grateful that I know what this is. I am going to be grateful. I don't want to allow it to cause me to behave in an angry manner. Now I am going to push it away from me and think of something positive. I refuse to let it take me down today. I'm staying up!"

It was quite a journey and still is. But because I engage in physical fitness daily, it sets the tone for my day. It sets the tone for my thinking and my loving. It wasn't until I committed to a full-on lifestyle that included fitness, did I grasp the concept of just how much my exercise regime helps me make wise decisions about most anything every single day. The clarity in my brain is phenomenal.

Exercise comes in many forms and it is different for everyone. But there is one thing you have to accept: Until you start exercising regularly, you are not going to get into it. You will not have fun with it. You will not feel the benefits! I have heard so many people say things like, "I just don't like to exercise…" OK—I will give you that, but did you know that there was a time that I did not like to exercise? Yep—but once I started doing it regularly, my body and mind craved it. You have to try to get to the other side of it, and that usually happens with consistency.

You have to make yourself do it every day. Even if it is a 30-minute walk, 30 minutes of yoga, or 30 minutes of running, cycling—whatever. Just get moving. Make it a requirement or "me" time every day. You deserve this time and the benefits are huge. If you need others, hire a personal trainer. Your local gym can help you find someone or ask your friends. Go to classes with others or find meet-up groups. I have so much fun meeting my friends for running, hiking, swimming, biking—I love to move!

If you prefer to do things alone, do it. I can exercise either way, but I do better with others, which means I plan a lot of my workouts with others when I am not teaching fitness classes. Another thing—do not feel embarrassed or that you will stand out. No one cares what you look like when you exercise, and in most cases, you will find that someone will help you. What is important is that you are doing it. Swimming is my biggest challenge. I went through a period where it felt forced. I did not like it, but I had to do it since it was one leg of my triathlon races. Though it took time, I started to enjoy swimming because I practiced consistently; I started to look forward to seeing my friends in the pool. It is still my least-favorite sport, but once I committed to going to my Masters Swim class at the gym, I not only started liking it, I got better!

NOT TRYING IS NOT AN OPTION. WHATEVER YOU DO, DO NOT STOP. DO NOT LET ANYTHING GET IN THE WAY OF DOING THESE EXERCISES (UNLESS YOU HAVE AN EMERGENCY, OF COURSE!)

A huge part of a joy-filled life is having a continual process. I share information about continual improvement in #7. This is a must-do. It does not stop. Before you feel pressure about this, hear me out. What I am saying does not mean that you cannot stop and take some deep breaths. In fact, you should and often. But it is those deep breaths and those stops or rests or regrouping moments—whatever you need—that will help you keep it going. And you have to keep it going. That is where the fire is.

I want to make sure you know the difference between continuous improvement and continual improvement. "Continuous" means non-stop, without breaks. It is a continuous stream. And, yes, that is certainly magnificent and you will have some extended periods of time when you are in a good season filled with continuous momentum. But continual improvement is more realistic. "Continual" means that you improve with breaks between each next improvement. Usually great things will happen as well as some mistakes or areas that you may discover that are in need of much improvement. Without mistakes, we never see where improvement can be made. The idea is to get better by not making those same mistakes—continual improvement.

EXERCISE
New Way of Being: #2 Physical Fitness

You are going to make a plan right now!

1. What exercises are you going to do today? List at least two or a cumulative of 30 minutes or more, and include when and where you plan to do it.

2. What time are you doing these exercises? Be specific. Choose a time that you know will allow you to succeed.

3. Now, continue the rest of the week. Make the plan. Do the plan.

#3
Mindful Eating

The other side is that through it all, I knew I hated the way I was eating. I knew it was wrong. I knew it could not last forever and that it was wrecking my body and mind. I finally said "no" to that way of living (which IS NOT living) and began to understand food and how it works with my body.

#3
Mindful Eating

Here's a simple fact: We don't know how to eat. How to eat? Of course, we know how to eat! Actually, no we don't. Our culture doesn't understand simple things like how many times a day should we eat? What should I eat? Which diet? Real food—what's that? Organic. Not organic. How much? If I exercise a lot can I eat anything I want? It can be confusing but it doesn't have to be. However, eating mindfully takes practice.

Much like there is a direct correlation between your physical activity and your state of mind, there is also a direct correlation between the food you put in your body and your state of mind. Food is more than a meal or a snack; it is fuel. Food is energy. However, much of what we put in our bodies actually saps our strength and robs us of energy. The result is a weak body and exhausted mind that just can't take any more.

So if you're depressed and people are telling you to "snap out of it" but you're putting the wrong kind of fuel in your tank, it is going to be next to impossible to get back on your feet with any meaningful and consistently healthy lifestyle. Combining that with no exercise can leave you feeling hopeless, with no desire to change. But YOU CAN and YOU WILL!

It is crucial that you take some time to learn about the foods you are eating and do your best to choose foods that will give you a healthier body and mind. Do you know where your food comes from and the process it goes through to get to your plate?

The cleaner you eat, the better you will feel. Most foods are laden with chemicals to help preserve them and keep them from becoming disease-causing foods. What do these chemicals do to our bodies? They cause all sorts of problems. Our bodies need nutrient-dense food in order to thrive. If we give our bodies chemically dense food, the body will suffer.

Much of the problem lies in how we were raised, combined with the way mass-produced farming by large corporations has taken over our food supply. Many of these corporations work hard to find ways to produce as much food as possible with as little money as possible so that they can sell it to you as cheaply as possible. OK—the truth about our food is that much of it is junk; if you eat this food, your body will become filled with junk. Eventually, your body and mind will feel the negative effects.

Now is the time to rethink your food, and with the rise in digestive issues, it is more important than ever. Let's get back to the basics—let's eat real food that our bodies can digest and put to good use. If you eat food that is filled with nutrition, you are going to feel so good. That is how we want to feel, isn't it?

Your body is super smart. When you give the body what it needs, it uses it properly. In return, you get a clear mind and a disease-free body that is filled with energy! Food can be your medicine instead of prescriptions.

It is time to evaluate what you are eating and how much you are eating. You must become a mindful eater. Mindful means being aware. With practice, it becomes a natural way of eating and, ultimately, the way we were intended to eat.

I have so many people ask me how I eat the way I do. They will say things like, "I feel fine eating my pizzas and cupcakes." Then I ask, "Well, do you? Have you ever gone without those items for more than a few days?" You may not realize just how good you can feel until you eliminate bad foods from your diet.

Many are also curious about what I do when I eat at restaurants. At one time, it was very difficult for me. I would almost freeze at the thought of eating at a restaurant that I did not choose, since most restaurants do not offer healthy options, even though they make claims to such options.

●●●●●●●●

I had an eating disorder for many years of my life. I did not know how to handle food. I used it as an emotional suppressant—which, of course, was only temporary. The other side is that through it all, I knew I hated the way I was eating. I knew it was wrong. I knew it could not last forever and that it was wrecking my body and mind. I finally said "no" to that way of living (which IS NOT living) and began to understand food and how it works with my body. It took me a long time, and the damage that I had done to my body took a long time to heal. But I overcame all these issues. You can too. Your obstacle could be that you eat the wrong foods—it does not require an eating disorder to push you into learning how to eat in a healthy, life-giving way.

●●●●●●●●

OK—so let's get specific. A can of green beans, as in a can that you buy off the shelf at the grocery store, is not fresh. You could choose that can of greens beans or you could choose the fresh, raw green beans available in the produce section, which is where you should do most of your shopping. Those greens beans are two entirely different things. One of them offers much more nutrition than the other—obviously, the beans from the produce section.

You have to start going for nutrient-dense foods! Your body craves good food, and with some time, your mind will too. You have to decide now and make it happen. Done.

Life is all about choices. The choices you make are yours to make. Why are you allowing the wrong choices to stay in your life? Is it easier? Most people greatly dislike change; it makes them uncomfortable. Change is good! If you want to see and FEEL a difference, you have to make changes.

About portions—you must become aware of your portions. Most packaged foods have multiple servings, even the small, seemingly single-size versions, which often have two or more servings. Read the label! If you consume normal portions of nutritious foods, your weight will be perfect. You will not crave and overeat. I loved what a good friend of mine said one night after dinner "Kitchen is closed."

Yep—use your mind—make good choices and trust that you are going in the right direction.

EXERCISE
New Way of Being: #3 Mindful Eating

Here is an exercise to help you be mindful of what you are eating. List what you typically buy at the grocery store in the left column. Next to each item, write down a healthier option.

Example: breaded fish sticks (not so healthy) vs. fresh, wild-caught salmon (healthy). Do not leave any item out. If you buy chocolate, dark chocolate is a better option than milk chocolate (the darker, the better). If you are uncertain as to what the better option is, there are ways to find out: Use Google or ask at the wellness counter in your local market. You can also message me on my Facebook page, and I will do my best to get back to you.

#4

Long-term Goals

Each has a dream and a desire, but has to face challenges every single day to get there. Some days are easier than others. At some point, these people find themselves ready to change because they desire something more.

#4
Long-term Goals

Set long-term goals. Use short-term goals to get there.

It's one thing to worry about the future and that is not healthy. It is another to dream about the future, and THAT IS HEALTHY. It is not only healthy, it is a way to get you there. Your path may change along the way and things will happen that you did not plan for. But it is how you go in the right direction.

A huge part of the process is going to involve change, something I noted in the last chapter. That is one reason so many people do not even try. They don't like change—they like comfort. But how do we get better and stronger if we don't change?

Changes, if chosen wisely, create an opportunity for growth and the ability to overcome challenges. A pro-athlete does not become professional without going through tons of challenges and obstacles that may have held that athlete back at one time or another. But their strong desire (we will come back to this emotion) gave them the strength and encouragement they needed to push ahead. That process is not much different from a successful entrepreneur, a stay-at-home mom, a business executive, or an author. Each has a dream and a desire, but has to face challenges every single day to get there. Some days are easier than others. At some point, these people find themselves ready to change because they desire something more.

OK—so you have a strong desire and it is pretty powerful. BUT, if you do not act on that desire, you are staying at status quo.

Now that you get the idea behind desire and action, let's get specific about long-term goals. Long-term goals are usually defined as something big that you are working towards achieving. This can be a business goal, a fitness or wellness goal, a personal goal for your family (like owning a home), starting a special meet-up group, writing your first book (or second or third etc.), or launching a non-profit organization...the ideas are endless. But what is right for you and YOUR WHY is what you want to think about.

So make a list. Do it now. Prioritize it. That's the first step!

EXERCISE
New Way of Being: #4 Long-Term Goals

List every long-term goal you can think of—no restrictions. Simply write it down in the workbook section of this book. Then prioritize each one by placing a number next to each goal. Number one is your top desired goal. Allow this to flow. It will change over time, but for now, just let it come to you and write it down.

#5
Dream Big

In that moment, I felt sad for her. I wanted to express how the energy of having goals transforms you. It drives you. It provides an abundance of life-giving excitement! I cannot imagine not having goals and dreams.

#5
Dream Big

I recently had a conversation with someone about goals. I asked her what her goals were, and she said she didn't have any. She was content. In that moment, I felt sad for her. I wanted to express how the energy of having goals transforms you. It drives you. It provides an abundance of life-giving excitement! I cannot imagine not having goals and dreams. And I love to surround myself with others who feel that same way. These goals provide so much joy. In my life, the goals are not just work related. They are related to my fitness activities, to my home environment, to my own behavior!

●●●●●●●●

Changing the way you think about goal setting can change your life in big ways. To set those goals, you've gotta dream big. The bigger you dream, the bigger the reality of that dream becomes. If you think you can just sit back, chill out on the sofa, and all this magic will just appear, you could not be more wrong. I don't know how many times I have felt frustrated because I allowed precious time to slip right by me.

I want to be clear—while big goals and dreams should be a part of your vision, the magic that you may want can be as simple as spending more time with your family, for example. The idea is to get specific about whatever the goal or dream is. The question is what kind of time? Is it quality time? (I hope so.) Then get specific. What are you doing with that quality time? Is it something the whole family will enjoy or only you will enjoy? You may have more success, and get to do it again, if it is something the whole family enjoys.

Another perspective is you may have a huge dream, such as starting a non-profit to end world hunger. Maybe you have a vision of starting a business of some sort. How are you going to do that? Start dreaming, and then take action.

Learn from the best. Research, read, talk, get mentors, and become deeply involved in like-minded organizations. In most cases, those people that you see as the best of the best did all of this at some point. And they stay on top of it every day. They do not let up. They choose to take steps towards their dream.

Many people compliment me about my business accomplishments and my success in racing and fitness. I am appreciative of those compliments, but I believe that anyone can do what I do and more.

I worked for these rewards. I will always be a student, striving to achieve my dreams. Yes, I am most certainly a driven individual. I have a ton of desire. I work hard for what I want to achieve. But there are areas where I need to work even harder.

I bring awareness to that and contemplate how I can get there. I write my goals down and think through the steps. It helps remove some uncertainty, but keep in mind that the uncertainty helps fuel the fun and mystery of it all. We live in a world where we want the answers to be given to us without our having to work for it. I have a ton of questions that I need to be answered too! By allowing space for the answers to come to me, the ones I need in that moment come—always.

● ● ● ● ● ● ● ●

I want to share something that people often do not realize. I have failed. I have failed many times in pretty much every area of life. Some failures were big. Some were small. But they were failures. And most successful entrepreneurs and athletes out there have experienced the same. That failure gives them the gumption to kick butt and try even harder and smarter next time.

I don't really like the word "failure"—or I don't like the negative connotations of the word. But recently I used it while telling someone about one of my start-up businesses. It actually felt good to describe my experience as a failure! Acceptance is huge. It takes us from that place of FEELING LIKE A FAILURE to BEING A CHAMPION—it can push us to persevere. Champions do not give up. They keep going. That is my definition of perfection. Being perfect is not the perfection that society builds; being perfect is always trying to be better and stronger with what you've got!

● ● ● ● ● ● ● ●

This brings us to fear. Fear holds many people back from even starting. I am not talking about fear of heights and that sort of thing. I am talking about fear of failure. Fear of what others think. Fear of what others will say. Here's the deal: FEAR IS NOT REAL. It is something YOU have conjured up in your head—YOU are allowing it to fester. The longer you neglect what's possible, the more fearful you become. But this type of imaginary and negative thought is holding you back from your dreams. Again, FEAR IS NOT REAL, but letting it hold you back is real if you allow it. Everyone has the potential to be EMPOWERED. Do you want that? I sure do!

Dream big. It is the only way to get there.

EXERCISE
New Way of Being: #5 Dream List

This exercise may seem a bit like the previous one, and it is OK if you have duplicates here. Think this way—if your #1 goal in the previous exercise is to buy a house, your #1 goal here might be to buy a 4,000-square-foot house on a farm with views of the mountains. This is sort of like a vision board. That will be the next step.

In the workbook section #5, or on a poster board of some sort, create visual imagery of your visions and dreams. Place photos, drawings, or words of your vision that show who you want to be and how you want to live in this world. Note that I am asking you to show WHO YOU WANT TO BE. Don't lose sight of that. Who you are is far more important than things, but including things that you desire for yourself and your family is fine. Just make sure to include what you see yourself doing too.

Where are you? Are there mentors that you love? A view from the home that you want? A dream job? Life-enhancing experiences, such as your family on vacation somewhere special? It can be as simple as thinking of yourself as a person filled with kindness. How do you show that? Helping someone? Kind thoughts? Put it all here!

You can clip photos from magazines, print from the Internet, draw illustrations, use words, or a combination. Just let it flow. You can always change it. The purpose is to see it. When you see it, you can be it! WHO DO YOU WANT TO BE?

#6
Play Big

I explained that having the vision and desire is great and what you need, but you have to take it a bit further. When the negative chatter and excuses start, stop them. You have the power to do that. I use it every day and love it!

#6
Play Big

Let's get serious! If you want the big dream, you have to play big for it. I liken this to training. Everything we do in life is like training for a big athletic event. Those athletes who get on the podium of a race, especially the pros, do not get there in a day. They train for it. They learn. They work with coaches. They get up two or three hours earlier than everyone else. They eat differently. Everything they do is with intention. Every workout. Every meal. Every race. All are done with specific intention and goals. They prepare. They do the work. And more often than not, if they do the work, they succeed on many levels. Why? That is how to play big. You get in there and you get really dirty! You work hard so that you can play with the best—or work your way up to it because eventually, you will get there IF YOU WANT TO.

To play big, you have to make smart decisions along the way. Those athletes make their own mistakes such as eating something they shouldn't the day before the race, or training too hard when they were supposed to have a rest day. Every decision will not be a good one.

What do you do with that? You learn from it. It's that simple. You take that information and apply it to your next situation. No one makes the right decision every time. No one. But everyone can make a better decision the next time. Everyone.

●●●●●●●●

A client asked me to coach them about their food choices and fitness. This person came to me saying they had had enough and wanted to make a change. I started talking to them about how to think about what they want. I explained that having the vision and desire is great and what you need, but you have to take it a bit further. When the negative chatter and excuses start, stop them. You have the power to do that. I use it every day and love it! Voices encourage you to skip the gym or that walk, to eat something that you know makes you feel unhealthy, or to take a shortcut while working on a task at work. You literally say to yourself, "Nope, I am not doing it that way, I am doing it this way, which makes me feel good, yields great results and I will be proud of that!" End of conversation. And then you do it!

•••••••••

One of the easiest things to do is say that we want something. Yet, often we say it without any real intention of doing it. In the #8 Way of Being, I share a lot about intention, but I want to go there a bit now. You must have the intention to make something happen. Then, act upon that intention. Be consistent! The moment you catch yourself acting in a way that is not in line with that intention, you have to stop it. Right then. THAT is where awareness becomes your best friend and takes you to places you have always wanted to go. Use it.

So PLAY BIG to get to the BIG DREAM. Break it into steps. Do research. Have intention. Meet the big influencers out there in your field or area of interest. Read. Learning from others and then making it your own is what's behind the true spirit of any self-development—business or personal.

EXERCISE
New Way of Being: #6 Play Big

Make a list of things you want to accomplish and the steps
for each that will get you there. Do this in a relaxed way. It
is just a list. Like the other lists, dreams, and ideas, it will
change. Allow it to flow, but try to think it through a bit.
When you break it into smaller steps, it is more attainable.
That is what we are after in this exercise.

#7

Continual Improvement

If you think you are done, you are far from it. In fact, you will never be done. Like me, you will always be a student. This is a precious, beautiful humble state of living.

#7
Continual Improvement

If you think you are done, you are far from it. In fact, you will never be done. Like me, you will always be a student. This is a precious, beautiful humble state of living. You may complete a chapter of your life, but you will never be done creating y.o.u. (your own utopia).

Life is about learning. To learn, we have to listen carefully. You have to pay attention to what is working and what isn't. You will make mistakes, and you should, because how else will you learn? You may have heard the phrase that it is OK to not be OK, but it isn't OK to stay that way. Take this seriously.

Sometimes we get into a funk and it takes what seems to be endless repeats of the same mistake. One example is diet. How many times have you decided to start that diet again? Alcohol is another one. Smoking. Shopping. The list is long. It can be a business decision or the way you handled an argument with your boyfriend, girlfriend, spouse, or co-worker.

We are a true work of art. Continual improvement leads us to a better life. And it definitely makes for an interesting life! But I want to be straight up about this—if you do not want to improve your life, you simply will not improve your life. Improving your life requires constant work. It is not easy either, but it gets easier. It ebbs and flows. Something that was hard becomes easy, but a new hard thing comes along to shake things up. What is great is that all those formerly hard things that you overcome will make you stronger. It goes back to the core of it all—continual improvement.

You have to build positive thoughts that stay with you. Going back to your goals and dreams, things may be holding you back that could be eliminated with a little work. Stop and think about what those things are.

Most of the time you know exactly what they are, but you don't want to admit it because you don't want to deal with it. It seems easier to keep things as they are because changing them means you might be uncomfortable for a while. That discomfort will take you to the next level. You have to toughen up a bit to go there. It is not as hard as you think, but you will make it harder if you do not make the choice, meaning you remain in a state of limbo. You are teetering on the edge. You wanna go, but it is too much work. Guys, the other side is so incredible, you will wonder what took you so long. So GO! Stop wasting time. MAKE THE CHOICE AND GO. DO NOT LOOK BACK. CHANGE YOUR LIFE WITH CONTINUAL IMPROVEMENT!

EXERCISE
New Way of Being: #7 Continual Improvement

Make a list of things that you do that bother you. Be super honest about this. It can be anything. Make the list on the left side of the page, and then note what you plan to do instead on the right side. How will you push it away, stop it, change the habit to something better?

#8

Set Your Intentions

This may be where you get confused and frustrated. Don't. Start with these 8 things, and the awareness of your purpose will envelop you in ways you never imagined.

#8
Set Your Intentions

We have now made it to #8 which actually circles back around, like the infinity shape that it is, to #1 since all of these Ways of Being are constant. Set your intentions. You must choose. What are you going to do with this life? What is your intention in this life?

This may be where you get confused and frustrated. Don't. Start with these 8 things, and the awareness of your purpose will envelop you in ways you never imagined. It is the most beautiful thing I have ever experienced, and what is amazing about that is that it will continue to happen on bigger and bigger levels.

Let's dig deeper. How do we set our intentions so that our intentions become who we are?

Let's think culture. You have probably heard of numerous companies that build their culture from within which oozes to the outside world. They build a brand, an image, and a way of thinking that together creates who they want to be.

Did you know that you could build your own personal culture? You can even build your family culture—and you should. You should take the time to understand exactly who you want to be, then be it by practicing behaviors that will help you become that person. That is your culture. Your very own personal culture.

What is great about this is that it guides you to make decisions about your behavior. It helps bring awareness to it. Over time, this behavior becomes very natural. One form of behavior that is super important is how we respect and treat others. When we respect others, regardless of how they treat others, it makes us a much better person and builds loads of character.

Confidence. Do you realize how important this is? However, there is a difference between confidence and ego. What you want is confidence that is defined by your culture yet completely humble. We will always face moments of uncertainty, but if you check in with that culture (which will reshape itself as you grow), you will quickly regain your confidence because your decisions are based on those principles.

Another side to this is to remember that while your decisions may be great, that doesn't mean decisions or ideas of others are not great. It could mean that it is just another perspective that is also very good and worth noting, paying attention to, and possibly implementing. We tend to live in a world that wants to feel as though OUR decisions are the best and the only good ones worth doing. That is not true. But your decisions can be great most of the time.

For the ones that are not great, ditch 'em and look for new ones. Own it and move on in pursuit of a better option. As I noted earlier, it's OK to not be OK, but it isn't OK to stay that way. The sooner you move away from the stuff that you know is not healthy for you, the better. And this could be anything from something you eat, overeating, to staying in a bad relationship, a relationship of disrespect, and on and on. Countless decisions can be bad, and most of the time you know they are bad. So get away from them.

Space. With all of this comes space. In order to make an impact through thinking or doing, you have to make space for it. If you have chosen a new way of thinking, and I hope you are inspired to do so by now, you have to make space for that new thinking. You have to be aware of the thinking you do not want. Push it away and allow the new thinking to come to you. This takes practice, but the first step is acknowledging it. If you do not see it happening, how can you push it away from you? You can't.

Practice. Be in tune with your actions. If you can stop a behavior that you know to be in poor judgment, stop it. Acknowledge it and decide what the new behavior is— what is the new culture? If the behavior already happened, do the same thing, which is to decide what the behavior should have been according to your culture. However, if an apology to someone is in order, lean on your humble self and do that too. Humble is good. Confident egos are good. Cocky egos are not good and will just get you into trouble.

Discipline. This is a must. Without discipline, obtaining new ways of thinking is going to be a bigger challenge. Discipline helps guide us to accomplishments. Use it by focusing on your intention for each and every day. If you catch yourself behaving in some way that is not part of who you want to be or trying to skip an action step that you had planned for the day, stop it immediately and get back on track. This is part of the practice of new behavior combined with action. Mistakes will happen. All you have to do is jump back on the path right away!

Gratitude. Through all of this comes the most important behavior. Gratitude must be a part of who you are. You must recognize the beauty in your life—even on the hard days, (actually, more so on the hard days). It is when you stop and see what gifts are in front of you during a tough moment that you will truly enrich your life, and the lives of others, as you move through it.

Mindset. The collection of all of these thoughts and behaviors is your mindset. It is you who has to choose your mindset. Some things are obvious, such as not lying, not cheating, and so on. But the way we think, which dictates the way we behave, is summed up in our mindset. You have the power to make this what you want it to be. The first step is deciding what you want it to be. The next is doing it every day so that it becomes natural to you. The last step is to continually evolve into "a better you" by recognizing what works and what doesn't, and then applying new practices to reshape your culture as needed. Have a vision and drive that vision. You are the only one who can.

Hope. Hope is a gorgeous word that shows promise and drive. It shows desire and love. It shows kindness. Always keep hope close to you and use it to guide you. You can hope your dreams to life through action. Hope for the very best possible—not just OK, but the best situation, behavior, effort or outcome possible. You do that by choosing to give everything you've got to get there.

Love. I want to end with love, which is where we started. Love is the most precious of all. It comes from a genuine heart. You must love to make progress. You must love to help this world. Change your mindset right now. Make love a part of who you are and how you live. You will be forever changed and will find peacefulness that is far richer than anything you have imagined. You will realize how things do not shape you, but that loving genuinely does.

Note the exact date and time of day in which you plan to implement this new way of thinking—your new mindset, your new culture. The date could be today! Why wait for happiness and freedom? YOU HAVE TO BE BETTER TO FEEL BETTER. IT IS THE 8 WAYS OF BEING THAT CAN GIVE THIS TO YOU. GO GET IT!

EXERCISE
New Way of Being: #8 Set Your Intentions.

Here is where you decide on your exact date and exact time to start this new lifestyle. Choose now. You have no reason to wait. Write it down in your notebook and commit!

Kyra Oliver
BIO

Kyra Oliver believes strongly in helping others, which is why she is an author and wellness educator who combines fitness, food, and a positive mindset to help people discover a *lifestyle that feels good.*™ She uses her work in her daily life as she trains for triathlons, marathons, and ultra distance trail races. She also teaches fitness classes and is a lifestyle coach.

Her concern for the world and the children in it led her to create the non-profit Hayes Foundation (www.hayes-foundation.org), named to honor her son, Hayes, who died at age four and half months of SIDS. She launched a successful national campaign This Side Up While Sleeping (www.thissideupcampaign.org), that delivers educational messages on a cute onesie to help reduce the risk of SIDS.

Meanwhile, Kyra continued to run her own award-winning company, Oliver Creative, helping clients build and market their brands, and eventually merged with a national PR firm. Today, Kyra continues to help others with her creative expertise as a consultant.

Kyra cares deeply about her relationship with God, as well as building her relationships with family and friends. She notes that "the influences we surround ourselves with help shape us." With her website called y.o.u. (your own utopia), (www.yourownutopia.com), Kyra shares ways for people to take care of themselves through recipes, workouts, DIY ideas, good reads, and, of course, living life with a positive mindset filled with love and kindness.

Workbook
and Journal

#1
Love

#2
Physical Fitness

#3
Mindful Eating

3

3

#4
Long-term Goals

4

4

4

#5
Dream Big

5

5

5

#6
Play Big

6

#7
Continual Improvement

7

#8
Set Your Intentions

8

8

8

Did you like this book?

I would appreciate it if you would post
a review via the page below:

http://amzn.to/2t7dpho

Thank you!

Kyra Oliver

Made in the USA
San Bernardino, CA
26 January 2020

63505350R00110